LET'S LOOK FOR COLOURS

Bill Gillham *and* Susan Hulme

Photographs by
Jan Siegieda

Methuen Children's Books

rainbow

felt pens are all colours
of the rainbow

red

red lipstick makes a funny face

yellow

look at Baby's yellow duck

green

green grass is fun to throw

brown

Jenny plants bulbs
in brown earth

orange

who wants an orange balloon?

blue

Jenny and Daddy are buying
blue flowers for Mummy

black

here is Jenny dressed all in black

white

white bubbles to wash your hair

pink

pink candyfloss at the fair

what colours can *you* see?

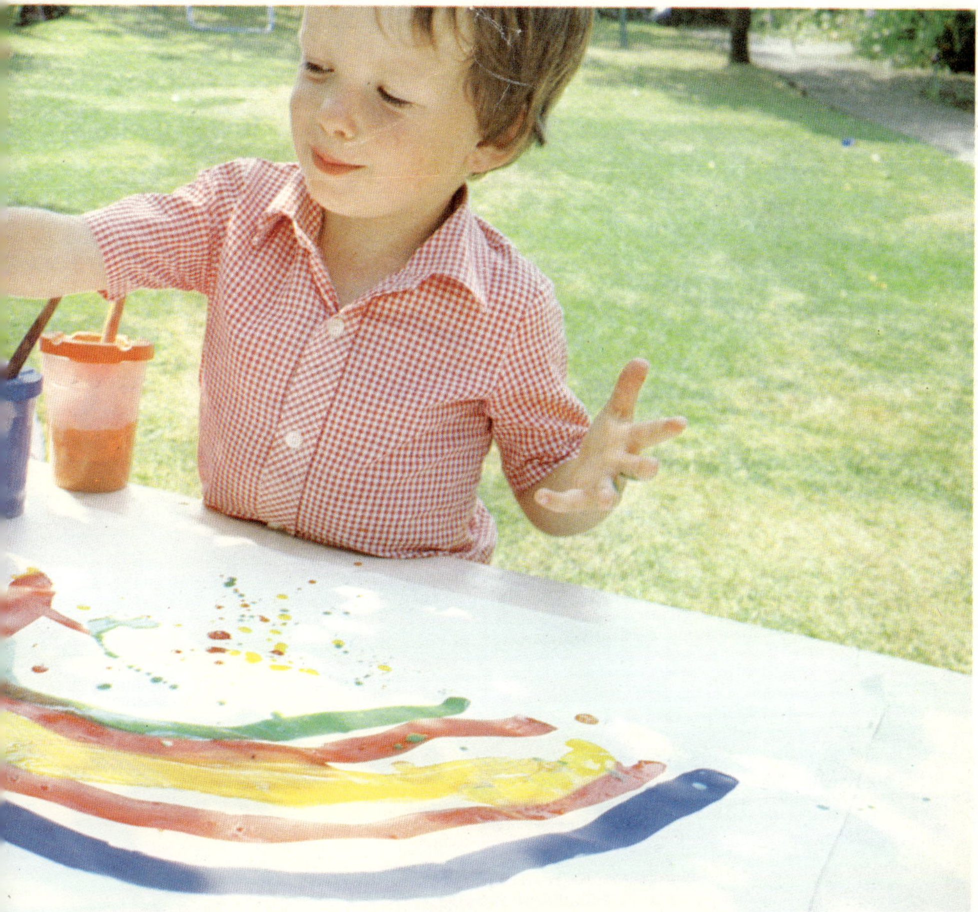

LET'S LOOK FOR COLOURS... is one of a series of four books designed to encourage children to *look* for the basic concepts of colour, shape, number and opposites in their everyday world. By talking around the topics illustrated, children will be encouraged to think of other examples and so to develop further their mastery of language and thought, quite apart from the intrinsic pleasure of sharing books with a 'helpful' adult.

Dr Bill Gillham is a well-known educational psychologist and children's author, and senior lecturer in the Department of Psychology at the University of Strathclyde.

Susan Hulme is an experienced infants' teacher, and mother of two young children, with a special interest in pre-school education.

Jan Siegieda is a freelance photographer; these are his first children's books.

Photograph of rainbow by Walter Leeson.

First published in Great Britain 1984
by Methuen Children's Books Ltd
11 New Fetter Lane, London EC4P 4EE
Text copyright © 1984 Bill Gillham and Susan Hulme
Photographs copyright © 1984 Bill Gillham and Jan Siegieda
Printed in Great Britain by
Hazell Watson & Viney Limited,
Member of the BPCC Group,
Aylesbury, Bucks

ISBN 0 416 46200 6